Labour
of
Love

Liz
Ragoút

LABOUR OF LOVE

LIZ RAGOÙT

LABOUR OF LOVE by Liz Ragoút © Copyright 2020 Liz Ragoút. All Rights Reserved and Preserved. No part of this book may be reproduced or transmitted in any form or by any means, electronic or mechanical, including photocopying, recording, or by information storage and retrieval systems, without written permission of the Publisher with exceptions as to brief quotes, references, articles, reviews, and certain other noncommercial uses permitted by copyright law.

For Permission requests, write to:
YBR Publishing, LLC
PO Box 4904
Beaufort SC 29903-4904
contact@ybrpub.com
843-597-0912

LABOUR OF LOVE

LIZ RAGOÙT

ISBN-13: 978-1-7339992-8-1

Bill Barnier – Senior Editor, YBR Publishing
Cyndi Williams-Barnier – Production Editor, YBR Publishing
Jack Gannon- Editor, Production Manager, YBR Publishing
Loreen Ridge-Husum – Art Director, YBR Publishing

LABOUR OF LOVE

LIZ RAGOÙT

"LABOUR OF LOVE"
Reviewed by Erin Nicole Cochran for
Readers' Favorite   readersfavorite.com

"Labour of Love" by Liz Ragoùt is a collection of poems that encapsulates her zest for life as well as her home and memories that stir within her. The narration that proceeds throughout the entire book is one that feels close to the heart. As a reader, you begin to sense your own connection to the places she describes so well. She paints her poems in such pictures that you can feel and smell the grass under your own fingers. Two of my favorite lines are on page 22 within the poem Little One's Dreams: "Where the sandman will catch / them in his gossamer threads." There's a beautiful, ethereal quality that each poem possesses, that brings you in deeper with every page that's read.

Liz Ragoùt's "Labour of Love" made me yearn for travel and days of summer. Though not all of the poems were solely centered on nature, some ranged from unique narratives, that I won't give away, to memories that were of warm heartache. Not completely sad, but full of appreciation for the time had and the time that will come again. Throughout the book, there are also images and illustrations of flowers and hillsides that bring an extra smile after the end of a poem. Liz Ragoùt's "Labour of Love" is a treasure that resides in an Irish girl's heart that she has decided to share with the rest of the world. It's a gem that everyone should see and get to feel. It is one for the ages.

LABOUR OF LOVE

LIZ RAGOÙT

Dedication

With Love from Great Granny for Ella Mae and Lainey Elizabeth Greenfield...

LABOUR OF LOVE

Acknowledgments

Sincere thanks to Deborah Brooks Langford of Wildfire Publishing for referring me to Cyndi Williams-Barnier and Jack Gannon at YBR Publishing, and to my son Seán Ragoút for his constant encouragement and support…

And special thanks to everyone at YBR Publishing for bringing my final book to life!

LABOUR OF LOVE

LIZ RAGOÙT

About the Poems

I do not consider myself an established poet, nor a great one at that, but I do pour my Celtic passion for all things emotional into my writings…

The span of my lifetime of 77 years is used in my poems from my earliest happy childhood, sudden death of my mother, descent into poverty, teenage yearnings, leaving my homeland, observations of nature, as well as life in general...

Hope for the future trips down memory lane, laments of an exile and communication with the universal mind and mother nature, are recurring themes.

The Poems speak for themselves as my love of God, home, family and the wider community shine through all…

LIZ RAGOÙT

Mothers Love

is a garden
where the Sun
always shines
and the season is
always summer...

LABOUR OF LOVE

Winter Blues

Winter approaches
with biting cold winds.
Its warm cozy kitchens
we want to be in.
We cough and splutter
all the way through,
eating warm stews and
battling with flu…
Christmas brings joys
for families with welcome
gifts, then tuck into roast turkey
and delicious plum pud…
The New Year brings hope
of better days to come,
as we toast it with whisky,
wine, ale and rum.
Later, we battle the North winds
and endure, until the first signs of
Spring, when snowdrops and daffodils
start poking through…
When the trees and hedges become
covered in beautiful green hues,
announcing the end to our shivering,
cold winter blues.

LIZ RAGOÙT

In Living Memory...

This summer in France
the cornflowers so blue
grew in profusion
to remind me of you.
At the foot of the Pyrenees
where we used to hike,
I stood to honour you and
your comrades,
who gave your all
for our freedom, without a
thought for yourselves...
Rest in Peace, my beloved,
we owe you our lives.
You will never be forgotten
until the last of us dies

LABOUR OF LOVE

Death by Humanity

The Honey Bees are dying
at the hands of man,
we must try and save them
any way we can.
Genetically modified Corn
is the cause of all the pain,
if people don't speak up soon
the Bees won't come back again.
The Monarch butterflies are dying
from infected plants and Maize,
weed killer spread on habitats.
please don't avert your gaze.
We must stop this wanton slaughter
and disregard for other species,
before our grandchildren
are deprived of nature's beauties.
And when the cycle of regeneration
halts its work anew,
the cause of the devastation
will be down to me and you...

LIZ RAGOÙT

Red and Green Peppers...

Having been brought up
on a farm in a convent,
we orphans had holiday chores,
picking potatoes, cabbage, swedes
and carrots,
as well as scrubbing the floors,
of course, our fingers and
backs got sore...
However, we never wanted
for foodstuffs,
having eggs and tomatoes galore,
as well as the root vegetables,
meat and potatoes, savoury stews,
bacon and creamy colcannon,
we could not have wished for more...
Yet I never ever had sampled
red and green peppers, savoury
baked beans or even spaghetti,
before I emigrated,
to England's pleasant green shores...
Now red and green peppers in onion and
Garlic, with Ragù sauce on pasta, and lots
of lovely mozzarella cheese, I adore......

LABOUR OF LOVE

Little Ones Dreams

Hush, said the night
to the wind,
so we can eavesdrop
on the whispering melody,
of innocent dreams...
Let's listen to the little heart
Beats, and the soft fluttering
of those tiny wings,
as they gently rise up into the
moonlight sky.
Where the sandman will catch
them in his gossamer threads,
to store in his baskets, to love
and protect them securely,
in the bye and bye.

LIZ RAGOÙT

Atoms

I am a tiny little twiddle
I can fairly wiggle and
you are important to me.
You can't see me, because
I hide behind my cloak of
invisibility…
1 and 1 still is one, 1+ 1 Is two,
and I am very important player,
as my extended family, makes you…

LABOUR OF LOVE

Daisy daisy

so delicate and white,
your slender beauty
is pure delight.
Awash with the mist of the
morning dew,
your fragile freshness.
is a joy to behold,
and your yellow crown
glistens like gold…
Daisy daisy, princess of flowers,
filling field and meadows with
happy showers, like fallen snow,
it's a pleasure to greet you
wherever you grow…

LIZ RAGOÙT

A Mind of Your Own

If you have ever wished
upon a star, seen pictures
in white fluffy clouds,
or walked in the rain in summer
to escape from the noisy crowds...
Chosen silence as a pleasure,
enjoyed the sounds of the ambience,
as you listened to the wheels of
the planet, gently humming,
and turning around.
It is then you would have discovered,
you are indeed, not a performing clone,
reflexively, rejecting suggestions,
you need to answer your phone,
because, You Do have a mind of your own.

LABOUR OF LOVE

What God Can Do...

The echo of the cosmic mind
rebounds throughout creation,
vast universes, spring eternal,
populated by its imaginations,
and tiny particles that created,
me and you.
When you see the twinkling stars
in the milky way, surely the elation
of creation wakes the wonder in you.
In the autumn leaves of colour made
by mother nature, you truly witness
what God can do...

LIZ RAGOÙT

Insight....

The fragrance
of juniper and roses,
blew by on the breeze,
as I sat on the beach,
watching the
evening tide come in.
The gentle ebbing and receding
of the turquoise sea, acted as a
a tranquillizer for my busy mind...
In a happy daze my thoughts
meandered about life,
the universe, and spirituality.
In my reverie I suddenly realized
I was indeed an important being,
playing an essential part in the
whole scheme of things.
I experienced a tiny spark of clarity...
As St. Paul once said,
"At first, we see through the
glass darkly,
then with insight, face to face..."

LABOUR OF LOVE

The Bigger Picture...

The universe doesn't
give you what
you think you need...
Instead you are amply
rewarded
for your thoughts and deeds.
The bigger picture that you
cannot see
remains a mystery.
Until at the appropriate
time
all will be revealed....

LIZ RAGOÙT

A Friend in Need...

Lay your head on my shoulder,
my friend, I'm not as weak as I
look, or too busy to care.
I'll hold you tight and safe for a
While, and give you some comfort,
maybe a little respite,
from the depression and the demons
that plague you at night.
I cannot promise to cure you, or even
know how, but am ready, here and
now, to support you until the dawn of light.
Until the fog that inflicts your dear mind,
settles down, and even after you access
guidance, of the professional kind, now I
want you to know, you are worth more than
gold, just continue to hold onto me…

Love Is....

The Mystery of love
is greater than the
mystery of death,
wrote Oscar Wilde,
the great Irish poet
a century ago.
Phil and I loved and
laughed a lifetime,
then he passed...
I still feel his love all
around...
I believe he's now part
of the mystery of Love

LIZ RAGOÙT

This Living Universe...

The universe pulsates
with life,
It is written in the rings
of trees,
In the pattern of petals,
and seashells,
and in the sounds of water.
In the rising and
setting suns, fresh morning
dew, bird song and the
babies first cry...
As twilight lingers
the stars begin
to twinkle and shiver,
they tremble and shine
like jewels,
and in my heart I know
I am a part of those stars
as are all of
the galaxies, and humanity.
We are the creation of this
magical living universe...

LABOUR OF LOVE

Way Back When… (Prose)

Sometimes this poet
yearns for those childhood days,
that are now since long gone.
To hear Mama singing as she
did the washing on the washing
board, the splash of the water as the
tin bath overflowed.
The voices of loved people, and the
touch of Dada's hands on her brow
all now lost in the ether,
somewhere, somehow…
The sweet smell of the meadows
when the men cut the hay, the
sound of the threshing machine
from far away.

The friendly banter of the men,
when we brought their lunch, of
great chunks of bread and cheese,
all washed down with gallons of tea.
Or the hours of laughter and fun in
Grannie's kitchen making current buns.
Oh, how I loved roaming the green
Hills with Grandad, hearing the stories

LIZ RAGOÙT

of when he was a boy, while learning
how nature provided the cycle of
seasons, so life could proceed as it should.
How when cultivated corn grew ripe, for
Harvest, then planted again to rise up once
more, after resting underground.
Oh, how I wish I could spend a while back,
when life was so happy, innocent and fun...

My Sanctuary

When the world overwhelms me,
and I'm feeling blue,
there is a special exercise I like to do.
Gazing into the gentle flame of a candle,
I visualize that I'm sitting by a stream,
in a wildflower meadow, watching the
water tumbling, over the stones...
Soon my mind grows quieter, my breathing
slows, I have left the darkness, now I go
into my sanctuary, and goodness flows into
my soul, then peace and tranquility grow.
I return refreshed ready to take up the reins
of daily life, knowing I can always go back,
whenever I am weary again...

LIZ RAGOÙT

Lifetime Allegiance...

Her demure smile, so innocent
and pure, reminds me
of summer and blue azure skies.
The magic continues throughout
time, since I fell in love with this
daughter of mine...
When she gazed at me with her
gorgeous green eyes, that were wise
with wonder, and the power to love...
This bundle of joy enticed my allegiance,
her every wish to fulfil, as did her brother
and sister before, I'm in thrall to them still.

LABOUR OF LOVE

Tender Recall...

Tender are the memories of Ratlin island,
where it seemed all the birds in Ireland
have a jamboree, as we walked its wild
and rocky paths in those hazy summer days.
Just a ferry ride from Ballycastle by the sea,
it was once part of the Dal Riada kingdom,
seat of the kings of Ulster, the fiery UnNeil...
The homeland of St. Columbia before he left
and founded the famous seat of learning,
Iona, the resting place of peace and solitude,
for many Irish Kings, tender memories indeed...

LIZ RAGOÙT

Strange Times

We are living in
strange times, half the
world is dying, all across
the globe
starving children are crying,
in war-torn towns and cities,
in our day.
To ourselves we continue lie,
as we go on to buy, more and
more commodities,
stocking up for a rainy day,
most of which will be thrown out
as trash, and taken away.
The lungs of the planet are burning
Brightly in Venezuela and Brazil,
terrified families living still in Syria.
And all the while, people smile and
employ the internet to convey their
regrets, nothing much has changed yet.

LABOUR OF LOVE

Sunny Day...

Today is the 15 September,
2019...
in leafy Barnet it's a beautiful
warm sunny day...
It seems the weather is trying
to pretend that summer is not
exactly over, as the soft perfume
of late roses fill the air, and white
butterflies flutter around...
The sort of day when miracles
and magic can easily happen,
laughter is not far away, and the
warmth of the Sun heals your heart.

LIZ RAGOÙT

My Beautiful Lady

Often in the quiet of the evening
when the twilight fireflies glow,
there is a secret place in my little
garden, where I love to go…
Here I receive spiritual inspiration,
that flows through my body and
mind, soft waves of love gently lapping
overflowing my soul…
This is a gift from my Lady Wisdom,
companion of my Father, The Lord.
The universal Mother of creativity,
first Apostle of Apostles, she who
knows the sacred mysteries of heaven,
of renewal, rebirth and recall,
Radiant loving teacher, awakening
the divine in us all….

LABOUR OF LOVE

The Spirit of Nature...

Mother Nature works
day and night,
steering the seasons
for our delight.
The virgin snows of winter,
harbour the seed of renewal
in the warm earth below,
even as the cold winds blow.
Springtime bursts through in
blossoming glory,
our hearts are elated to see
the birth of this story.
Summers sultry days beguile us,
with sunshine, sand, other countries,
as we plan our holidays in exotic
locations across the seas...

Autumn arrive in blazes of colour,
on meadows, hedges and on trees,
harvest time is almost over, the
yearly ritual is over, if you please...

LIZ RAGOÙT

Mystery Of life

Sometimes I feel
like a shadow,
flitting between the
earth and the wall.
I'm often very little,
other times I walk tall,
and sometimes
I'm not with it at all.
I look at myself
with wonder, and seek
answers, for the meaning
of this strife.
Then I discover many
others experience these
moods of depression, as
part of the mystery of life.

LABOUR OF LOVE

When I was Snoozing...

I was stolen from a field in Kildare Ireland
to be a status symbol for a family of Jones,
my parents are unknown ...
so, at first, they didn't class me as pedigree.
They soon changed their minds when
I started winning point to points...
Being social climbers, they had the great idea
of enrolling me to race on the flats as Duke,
before that I was just Rowena's horse.
After I won a few races, they sold me like a
Slave, to the O' Paddy Stud in Bray...
It was nice there, the stable lads and lassies
were very kind and gentle and I got a trainer
of my own, Brian O' Breen...
To cut a long story short, I won the
Cheltenham gold cup and the Grand National.
Then I woke up to find myself back in the field.
Away with ye, a fellow can dream, can't he?

LIZ RAGOÙT

Pass It On

The smallest
act of kindness
is like
a mustard seed
scattered
on the ground.
Pass it on...
It can take root
and spread
like wildfire
bringing joy to
countless unknown
people.
Pass it on...
To those who live
in loneliness.
a smile, a chat, a hug
a helping hand of
human warmth,
is like a healing balm...
Pass it on...

LABOUR OF LOVE

Wildflowers

In the midst
of the turmoil
of daily strife,
on the way home
from working all
day ....
You catch a glimpse
of heaven
as the Sun is setting,
a meadow of
wildflowers that delight
your senses.
You feel the hassle of
the day easing of
your shoulders and fading
away, as you drink in
the sudden beauty that
has come your way...

LIZ RAGOÙT

Four Faces of Me...

I was christened
Elizabeth at birth,
then Lily for short,
intermingled with
shouts of Elizabeth
for officialdom sake.
Entering student nursing,
too many Elizabeths there,
so, I became Liz unawares.
Later in life, as is the way
seniors are perceived,
I became Lizzy one day…
That entitlement is now here
to stay, except it's Elizabeth on
the mortgage, council bills, wills,
and the countless junk mail that
keeps coming my way.
I do prefer Lizzy I must say…

LABOUR OF LOVE

Lest the World Forget...

At the onset of
the holocaust,
the sword of power
was used
to slay moral justice.
The concepts of hope,
fairness and
balance, was trampled
underfoot,
cast into darkness
and decay.
The deliberate murder
of millions
of innocent men, women
and children
saw decency, rationality
and pity,
the moral ethics of law
and order, cast into outer
darkest, depravity and
vile murderous obscenities…
Lady Justice
slowly returned after
many millions of lost souls

LIZ RAGOÙT

faded away...
The allies eventually
lighting the lanterns again,
restoring the ideals of the
rule of the law,
and the powerful memory,
of an unholy war, that would
stain the whole world forever.

Inspiration

When the flame of
inspiration ignites
the imagination,
there are no limitations
to the expressions of
poetic minds...
Mystery and magic
Intermingle, setting the
spirit free, to sail the seas
of wonder, and roam
among uncharted realms,
amid strange happenings.
Travelling through shadow
lands and sunlit meadows,
telling tales of joy and
woe, sagas of troubled
hearts, long lost loves and
memories of the long ago...
Always in those flights of
Fancy, to express opinions,
and rekindle fires of rosy love,
sad poignancy, awakening,
echoes of the children's laughter,
music to refresh the soul.

LIZ RAGOÙT

Déjà Vu

It was a relief to escape
the intense heat, as I slipped into a pew
in the quiet country church.
I gradually became aware of an intoxicating
smell of roses, lilies and sweet pea.
It was a kind of spiritual aroma, a sign I thought,
a gentle remainder,
from another world, of peace and tranquility.
I had been born a Catholic,
before lapsing from the faith of my father's.
I knew my wasteland was peopled,
by the ghosts of all those who had somehow,
contributed to my desertion.
But here in this simple setting, the ambience
was serene, as shafts of ruby light, from the
stained glass windows pierced the shadows,
and whispered memories of long ago, hung in
the air, like incense…
I became aware of an intense feeling of Déjá Vu.

Easter Sunday

Breath of
my breath,
light of my life
He was
no ordinary man,
but a special son,
sent from paradise.
Who died for
no other other
reason,
other than,
every spring season,
we would be
reminded,
that he
survived the grave,
so that
we might live.

LIZ RAGOÙT

The Call of the Sea

As I grew up on an island,
I have always been captivated,
by the rhythmic nature of gentle,
breaking waves, and long happy
days, spent splashing by the seaside.
The lure of the never-ending freedom,
of the vast, wide open spaces, sailing
the ocean appealed to my wanderlust.
Being unaware then of the ferocity and
powerful force of an angry sea.
Nevertheless, I have grown to love and
respect the mighty oceans, and be fascinated
by the sounds and songs of the sea birds,
soft breezes, and stories of mermaids, and
unexplored, underworld creatures of the sea.

Mystical Light

We live in a simulation,
a virtual world,
where we can tune into
energies and tones,
higher harmonics of a
vastly different kind.
We can experience vibrations
and frequencies
at the speed of thought,
with our own minds.
Consciousness is the
only reality in this place.
Sound and light travel
in waves through space,
and if we study light
through misty water, we can
see that rainbows, are light
travelling with us, and if we
take time, we will also
see a bridge there, that we
didn't notice before.
The true door to freedom
is through ourselves.
Knock and it will be opened,

LIZ RAGOÙT

seek and you will find
the key to unlock
the door to the divine.
It has already been written before,
for the benefit of mankind.
You can access it anytime,
through the power of your mind.

LABOUR OF LOVE

In the Summertime

The kindest heart
I ever knew,
shared his love and life
with me.
The years have flown
swiftly by,
It seems like only
yesterday,
he sailed away on the
celestial sea...
In the summertime...
His soft voice always low
and kind,
echoes melodious in my
mind, his laughter,
deep as tumbling waters,
and his kisses,
sweet as barley wine, remain
with me.
I used to grieve, now I celebrate
our love...
in the summertime.

LIZ RAGOÙT

True Love

The spark of true love

never dies,

but changes course,

throughout our lives,

always faithful, always true…

Enduring, separations,

strife and pain.

Real Love has the power

to heal again.

The strength of your love

has sustained me,

through many happy,

and the darkest of days.

The touch of your hands

and the love in your eyes,

lead me to understand…

That even in death,

true love like ours, never dies.

LABOUR OF LOVE

New Jerusalem...

Our majesty Sun, surrounded,
by its children, the planets,
is the centre of our solar system,
a shining lamp of illumination
and the spirit of our world.
The universal mind has assigned
Father Sun and Sister Moon, to
Mother Earth, to nurture creation
towards spiritual transformation
and maturity.
In order that our minds be elevated
to understanding our existence,
igniting our soul consciousness,
so we may be resurrected among
the stars in New Jerusalem...

LIZ RAGOÙT

The Magic of Water

When I was a youngster
I often used to play,
beneath the waterfalls
almost every day.
I loved to see the sun
go down over the ocean,
on Ballycastle bay.
The wonder of those
happy days have
always stayed with me.
I'm fascinated by water,
be it river, rain, or sea,
I like to see raindrops sliding
down the window panes.
Running waters hold such good
memories, of how life used to be,
when we lived as a happy little
family by the Irish sea...
I even enjoy walking in the rain,
as the magic of running water,
still captivates me.

LABOUR OF LOVE

Peace of Mind

In the midst of these
hard and troubled times
when the nations are
undergoing great divides…
It's a pleasure to steal a few
peaceful hours, in a shady
glen by a babbling stream.
Oh, how wonderful it would be
if we could all relax in the
shade of the trees, without
the worry of wars and dissent,
the state of our world and how
it has changed in these later times.
Oh, for solitude and peace of mind.

LIZ RAGOÙT

Fate and Family...

In 1960 I came across
the Irish sea,
a partially deaf village lass
straight from convent life.
An orphan from an early age
I was now seventeen...
Hearing aids helped me to settle
into the nurses' homes' social life,
being made welcome enhanced it.
I was befriended by a nurse who
introduced me to the man who was
in time to change my life.
Philip grew up in London after his
parents moved down from Newcastle,
he was a second-year student nurse.
After graduation, we married, had three
children who, like me, will always remember
Philip with much love and affection. R.I P.

Visions of Love...

Walk the highways and
byways of Ireland,
drink in the visions of love,
that Mother Nature presents,
leased from the owner above.
Ireland is known as the land of
Guinness of saints and scholars
galore, music, poets and dancers,
and storytellers new and old.
God's own acres' fame is renowned

LIZ RAGOÙT

Another Dimension

As children we played a game,
Don't walk on the cracks in the
Road, else you'd slide in.
Even today at 76 I still don't walk
on the cracks in the road,
regardless what anyone watching
will say, I don't care to this day.
Back then I used to wonder what
I might find, if I really did slip through.
My brothers said we'd end up in the
sewerage system, which made us girls
doubly-extra careful indeed.
Nowadays I think I would just slip into
another dimension, and I find it a little
scary, but exciting all the same.

LABOUR OF LOVE

The Power of Prayer...

In the midst of the noise
War and death
There is wonder contained
In a child's breath.
In the sound of prayer
Sincere and true
You'll find the answer
To what you can do.
Hope for the future,
Help for a friend.
In a simple prayer
Love without end.

LIZ RAGOÙT

You Are Precious

When your heart is heavy
and your spirits feel low,
the world overwhelmingly
full of shadows,
for a walk you should go.
Get in touch with nature
for she is ever ready to show,
that what you're experiencing is
an imbalance in the fast flowing
river of the waters of life.
Attune your thoughts to the natural
world, with an awareness of how the
seasons continue to wax and wane,
come hail, thunder, snow and ice, then
bright sunshine again.
Remember to stay in touch with your soul,
whether you are rich, poor, young or old, for
you are a child of the universe, as precious
as the star's in the sky, the sun and the moon,
in the universal mother Goddess's eyes.

LABOUR OF LOVE

Born in The Work house

I was born in the workhouse
in Daisy Hill Newry in 1942...
Witness to my birth was one
Mrs. M A McCormack who signed
herself as an Inmate,
This was the polite address of one
who actually resided there.

This lady was my grandmother,
my father was named as a street
musician (he played a melodeon),
Michael McAvoy of Warrenpoint Rd.
This desirable address was a tent
on the side of the road near
Narrow Water Castle, Newry Co. Down...

The work house was for the destitute
of the parish, until it was revamped
and transformed into wards and clinics,
with cozy lounges and coffee tables,
to became one of the first National
Health Hospitals in Northern Ireland
in 1948...

LIZ RAGOÙT

Our mother and grandmother died in that
place over the years 1946 and 1953.
I'm told it was still run as a strict regime of
austerity until well after its inception…
I have long wondered about the fate of the long
time destitute, and vulnerable folk, who originally
found refuge in this stark last chance saloon…

LABOUR OF LOVE

Sublime...

Sitting alone in the quiet
of the evening,
my thoughts gently turn
to my state of mind...
My breathing gets slower,
my heartbeats grown softer,
as I dwell on my soul,
and contact the part of me,
that is in touch with the divine...
Non-verbal contact is then
established, soon I feel,
I am outside of time,
at peace with such beauty that is
always sublime...

LIZ RAGOÙT

Rejoice in The Light...

Now as the nights draw in, it's getting dark earlier and as the cold days of winter close in around us, I'm reminded of the words of Genesis 2/3...

"The earth was without form and void, darkness was on the face of the deep, and the spirit of God hovered over the earth...
And God said, 'Let there be light,' and there was light..."

Every dawn when I watch the sun rising, I remember this passage, and I rejoice in the light...

LABOUR OF LOVE

Songs of The Sea

The winds on the waves
of the sea,
sound like music to me.
Rising and falling reacting
to hidden rhythms,
echoing on the oceans breeze...

The north winds blow in low,
low, angry and cold, howling.
like mad phantoms lost at sea.
Ghostly, shrill, their lament,
sad enough to frighten me.

The south winds sail in gently
across the waves, caressing
the sea with sweet murmurs,
and haunting melodies of ease.
singing happy songs that please.

The trade winds from the east,
bring warm tropical calm,
and a pleasant steady breeze.

LIZ RAGOÙT

Reminding us of summer days,
sailing round the bay...

The west winds sail serenely,
riding the crest of the waves,
their gentle ripples cascading
across the vast ocean wide,
promising warm embraces and
inviting lullabies...

LABOUR OF LOVE

Lady Light...

Children of the Sun,
may the hallowed Light
be glorified.

Eve, the idealistic first woman,
out of whose womb the world
was awakened.
She who wears the crown of
life, and the wreath of roses.
She is the radiant fertile vine,
mistress of the divine

Adam, the idealistic first man,
consort of mystical mind,
keeper of the hidden
powers, of her who bears a thousand times,
a thousand fruits, and ten thousand times
times ten thousand shoots...
Treasures that will mature in the
fullness of time...

LIZ RAGOÙT

Glory Be...

I once met an old man on the seashore,
nearly bent double was he, as the waves
of the stormy incoming tide, got nearer
and nearer, I feared for his safety.
Passing I reached out to aid him, as he
shuffled slowly past me, he looked up and
his eyes were shining, as he gently said to me.

"Thank you, child, for your kindness, one day
I will repay you double, nay on reflection I
will repay you thrice, your thoughts and actions
are noted, by my father in heaven, and me."
There on the evening seashore, that old man
ceased to be, in his place was an Angel, glory be...

These Are My Mountains

The ages pass and the
centuries flow,
the mountains remain,
the friends that I know.
They straddle the counties
majestic and grand,
the lovely Mourne mountains,
the pride of Ireland

These guardians of secrets
of the clans o'er the years,
are memorable treasures that
leave many an exile in tears.
The memory and beauty of these
 majestic friends, of good times,
I carry within me wherever I go,
sweet poignant reminders of home...

LIZ RAGOÙT

Wonder of Wonders...

Our planet hangs in outer space,
hard to believe it supports the
human race ...
Our ancestors didn't even realize,
their home was situated in the skies.

Today we know we are but one,
of the trillions of planets that orbit
millions of suns, in the vast galaxies,
that make up the universe, many of
the wonder of wonders that we inherit...
Will we ever learn to be worthy to join the federations of
the other worlds
that twinkle and swirl in the Milky Way?
Will humanity, in time, cease warring, agree
universal peace, and our maturity increase...

LABOUR OF LOVE

Tranquility

Sometimes I sit in silence
and let my mind roam free,
awaiting patiently,
until the sights, and sounds
of other days, in my reverie,
arise to soothe my soul.

Waterfalls and fields of golden
corn, awaiting harvest,
swaying like waves on water,
in the gentle breeze,
our old white cottage on the hill,
the silver sand on the seashore.

The blackbirds are singing in harmony
among the willow trees,
scarlet hedges, red with berries,
the emerald fields reflecting the sun,
and the busy little streams murmuring,
on their way to meet the sea.

While I, filled with nostalgia, view the
distance farmhouses,
and the orchards in the valley far below,

LIZ RAGOÙT

such pleasant scenes are nectar for my soul.
Then peace is restored within me,
I feel I can return to write again and find,
rhyme and inspiration, with ease.

I have stored this tranquility within
my heart, and use it now I know…
truly, the beauty of home and nature,
will always be nourishment for me,
as flowers are to the honey bee,
and acorns to the old oak…

About Fairies...

The fairies are dancing the dance of life
giving thanks for their lives, for husbands,
for wives, partners, children as well, sharing
their joy as happy folks do, and they include
me and you…

Fairies are older than old father time, they
have lived in the earth since creation.
A tolerant nation of a different kind who have
got a bad reputation from ignorant people with
a vested interest in mind.

Over the ages they have lived peaceful lives,
rarely interfering with earthly kind, unless to
rescue or defend one of their own…
They live between worlds on the edge of our vision,
and ensure invisibility except at exceptional times.

LIZ RAGOÙT

Age Is No Barrier

I recently looked in the mirror and
saw my real self, floating there,
my wings a-fluttering with the
breeze in my hair, as the autumn
leaves danced, and twirled around
me, frolicking merrily, in the fresh air...

I was happy from the inside out,
had no worries, had no cares.
After seventy-seven years on old
mother earth, I felt life is still
worth living, as I have given sin a
wide berth, I've been busy helping
others, and fostering peace.

Never fretting if my hair was getting
white, or my fleshy body becoming
wrinkled and old, for I know I have always
been careful, for my mortal soul...
Its inner glow shining a healthy light, to keep
me in pristine condition, until the time is right...

LABOUR OF LOVE

For All Souls Day

Every soul is part of
the one soul of the ineffable
love, of the divine, that sustains
all spirits on earth and when its
 their time, to leave this world...

Sometimes words are found
wanting, and we need to feel
we are not alone, in this vale
of tears, it's then, when the
least unexpected miracles appear.

A visible sign of the power of the
Love of the divine can be seen,
in the orbs of light that float around
when the individual soul exits the body,
and sets off on its journey to paradise...

Normally when a loved one has passed.
these orbs appear, dancing around the ones they loved,
in reassurance of their continuing existence,
and to leave loving messages of comfort and peace...

LIZ RAGOÙT

Remember Them

Tread softly as
you pass along this way,
remember I was alive
and young one day.

Forget me not
because I've gone away,
my Spirit lives
it's just my body that decays.

Remember me and all
that passed this way,
who gave our earthly lives
so you could live today.

Dwell softly on
our memory,
lest you forget the awful price,
we youngsters had to pay.

LABOUR OF LOVE

Secret Garden

Roses grow in midwinter
in a place I cannot name.
it's a secret little haven
from terror, hate and shame.

In this secret garden
I often stop to share,
my thoughts with wiser people,
who are always waiting there.

They plant the seeds that flourish
in that ethereal realm
so we can live in harmony
when they are at the helm.

It's always free to enter,
just knock your inner door.
you know it will be opened
for you have visited here before...

LIZ RAGOÙT

A Raging Sea

It strikes me of a sudden,
a cruel raging sea,
to my discerning eye,
murders its living creatures,
in its revelry....

Death for them is merciful,
it comes but once and sets
them free...
In the darkness of the night
such thoughts occur to me...

LABOUR OF LOVE

Ballycastle Bay

Sometimes
I steal away,
from life's
niggling cares
and strife,
to daydream
of other days,
the happiest
of my life…

Where the
sunset turns the
rugged cliffs,
to shades
of golden hues,
that bounce
off the water,
in the soft
evening light.

The fuchsia
running wild,
along the
harbour wall,

LIZ RAGOÙT

seagulls screeching
happily
at the trawler's haul,
bobbing and diving
like dancing waves.

I picture the
blue mountains,
the little houses
on the hills,
lovely echoes
of other days,
of my childhood
by the sea,
in Ballycastle Bay…

LABOUR OF LOVE

In Praise of Mothers...

Mothers are the universal
backbone of the nations,
who nurture, care and nourish us
throughout every situation.
They are a cause for celebration.

In this world of contradictions,
mums are the staple force for good,
they shield us from afflictions
as only mothers could.
They are as essential to us as food.

A mother's love is a blessing
unconditional and true,
no matter what our troubles
she knows just what to do.
Mum is always there for you.

Respect and honour your mama,
even when's she's old and grey,
for you'll never miss her gentle love
until she's buried beneath the clay.
Keep her close and love her for,
she will be called away one day.

LIZ RAGOÙT

Memory Lane

How I love to wander down memory lane,
to see again the soft green Antrim hills.
I picture the purple heathers, and the wild
red poppies as they grow, and smell the
coconut aroma, of the yellow bloom.

I can feel the first kiss of summer on my
upturned face, while I watch the rabbits,
run in the golden cornfields, as they race…
I sense the smell, of the nearby silvery sea,
on the breeze, recalling how happy I used to be.

Wandering in these glen's in the long ago,
when the world was much safer, there was
nowhere we children couldn't go.
Oh, how I love to linger on daydreams, such
as these.

LABOUR OF LOVE

Glen Affric

You would have to
have a heart of stone
to stand up here and
not be moved by the
beauty of Glen Affric,
the highlands of
Scotland's loveliest glen.

Looking down the valley
you can follow the trail
of meandering streams
as they weave merrily along...
The setting sun is reflected
on the waters in an explosion
of beautiful colours.

A heart-warming picturesque
Scene, wistfully sad, with the low
song of the whistling wind, that
echoes the sound of the gurgling
waterfall, as it frolics and cascades
across and around, the rocks on
this holy ground.

LIZ RAGOÙT

Home Calling

I've wandered far, far from
my own native home,
seen many grand sights
in the lands I did roam.

Of all the fine places
I'd rather be,
it's home where my heart is
In the hills by the sea.

One day I'll return
to my dear Antrim glens,
to stroll by the waterfalls
be enchanted again,

by the lure of their magic,
it will be heaven to me,
to be where those hills,
sweep down to the sea.

LABOUR OF LOVE

Robin Redbreast

Every time I see a Christmas Robin
my thoughts return to you and
I recall with love and pleasure
the things we used to do.

Amid the winter gloom the festive
season is always a joy.
The magic of each Christmas
Is not just for little girls and boys...

The sharing and caring,
Goodwill to all mankind.
The Peace of each new Christmas
Is Something Divine...

I bid the little Robin welcome
and admire his bright red breast.
The times they may be changing
I like our special ones the best...

LIZ RAGOÙT

Journey's End

When I hear the sound of a river,
murmuring on its way.
It reminds of my home town and
Beautiful Ballycastle Bay.

When I pass the village of Cushendun
at the foot of the lovely Glendun,
that has a big bridge over the river,
when I reach it, I know then.

It won't take me long at all,
to get back to our cottage again.
A few short miles, round the bend
I will come to my journey's end...

LABOUR OF LOVE

About the Author

Liz Ragoút is now retired after a long career in the caring sector.

Irish by birth, Liz emigrated to London, England early in life and has established a home and family in the suburbs of that great city.

She is a lifetime lover of literature; however, Liz is a late-comer to writing.

Due to childhood meningitis she has always been hard of hearing. Liz credits this hidden disability to her having developed a deep sense of observation because of her need to be aware of people when in conversation. This talent has served her well with her writings.

www.ingramcontent.com/pod-product-compliance
Lightning Source LLC
Chambersburg PA
CBHW052111070526
44584CB00017B/2442